Roatan & Honduras' Bay Islands

Sharon Collins

Pisces Books™
A division of Gulf Publishing Company
Houston, Texas

Publisher's note: At the time of publication of this book, all the information was determined to be as accurate as possible. However, when you use this guide, new construction may have changed land reference points, weather may have altered reef configurations, and some businesses may no longer be in operation. Your assistance in keeping future editions up-to-date will be greatly appreciated.

Also, please pay particular attention to the diver rating system in this book. Know your limits!

Pisces Books
A division of Gulf Publishing Company
P.O. Box 2608, Houston, Texas 77252-2608

Library of Congress Cataloging-in-Publication Data

Collins, Sharon, 1956–
    Diving and snorkeling guide to Roatan and Honduras' bay islands / Sharon Collins.
        p.   cm.
    Includes index.
    ISBN 1-55992-074-2
    1. Skin diving—Honduras—Islas de la Bahia—Guidebooks. 2. Scuba diving—Honduras—Islas de la Bahia—Guidebooks. 3. Honduras—Islas de la Bahia—Guidebooks. I. Title.
    GV840.S78C55 1993
    797.2′3—dc20   93-17943
                                                                  CIP

Pisces Books is a trademark of Gulf Publishing Company.

Printed in Hong Kong

10 9 8 7 6 5 4 3 2 1

Table of Contents

Acknowledgments

This book is dedicated to my father, Warren Collins, from whom my love of the sea and its inhabitants originated and flourished.

I should like to acknowledge several people who helped make this book a reality: Helen Collins, my mother, who painstakingly edited and typed the manuscript; Hector Andrade, who encouraged me throughout the process; Ken and Kathleen Greenwood, who reviewed, critiqued, contributed photographs, and gave me moral support throughout; Gordon Dehler and Eileen Klein, who contributed their knowledge and photographs of the Bay Islands and assisted me in any way they could; and Bruce Chambers, Jane Ford, Kurth Chinn-Fatt, and Martin Patoka, for their photographic contributions. Numerous others shared their impressions and confirmed some of my information on dive sites.

How to Use This Guide

The Caribbean has long been recognized as a paradise for the adventurous traveler. Diving's increase in popularity in turn has increased the search for the spectacular diving experience.

A green jewel set in turquoise waters, Guanaja boasts breathtaking views from any vantage point. Photograph by K. Greenwood.

The Bay Islands of Honduras consist of 8 islands and 65 associated cays enveloped in peace and tranquility. The exotic names of these tropical islands roll off your tongue: Roatan, Guanaja, Barbareta, Utila, and Cayos Cochinos. Nestled against the northern coast of Honduras, these little-known islands offer some of the most fabulous diving to be found in the Caribbean. Breathtaking drop-offs stretch for miles in sparkling splendor, interrupted only by a few sea channels. Pinnacles are laced with black coral, a green forest in the mist of clear, startling blue waters. Colorful coral

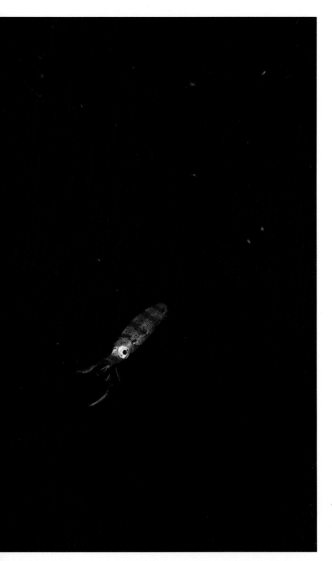

A Plee's striped squid ripples through the night waters, eyeing the photographer with curiosity. Photograph by B. Chambers.

gardens just a few fin kicks from shore tower with pillar corals. Shallow mini-walls grace the fringes of paradisiacal cays and abound with an exhibition of color and movement. To dive the Bay Islands is to visit an enchanting new world. Pioneer spirit, though not a requirement, is encouraged. Virgin reefs, never before explored, await the diver's pleasure.

The wealth of marine life has inspired the Honduran government to initiate a conservation effort. Several reef sites have been identified as potential marine sanctuaries.

Too often, a diver embarks upon a diving adventure ignorant of the complex array of dive sites available. Common post-dive conversations revolve around deciding the nature of animal or plant species observed. What is a brain coral? What was that brilliant blue-spotted fish?

This guide is presented to the diver and snorkeler as a reference to the more exotic and popular dive sites. Specific dive site locations, maps, and features are outlined for easy access, choice, and identification, whether diving on your own or through a resort operation. Valuable information is presented for planning diving activities in relation to physical conditions of the reef, currents, recommended expertise, and photographic considerations. An abbreviated marine life discussion is provided as an aid to "fish-guessing conversations" so that the diver may truly appreciate the wonders of the reefs. Several of the more common inhabitants are described for ready identification.

The Rating System for Divers and Dives

Whenever diving activities are proposed, consideration should be given to the limitations and expertise of the divers involved. As in any activity, a little common sense is useful in preventing potential mishaps. Therefore, although a dive site is rated for a specific minimal level, use the ratings to assess your own limitations and do not dive the site unless you are comfortable with the conditions presented therein.

A *novice diver* is one who is in decent physical condition, and (1) has recently completed a basic certification diving course, or (2) is a certified diver who has not been diving lately, or (3) has no experience in similar waters.

An *intermediate diver* is a certified diver in excellent physical condition who has been actively diving for at least one year following a basic course, and who has recently been diving in similar waters.

An *advanced diver* is someone who has completed an advanced certification diving course, is in excellent physical condition, and has been diving recently in similar waters.

There is a diversity of reef structures in the Bay Islands, ranging from offshore sheer drop-offs to the calmer inshore and shallower sloping reefs. All divers should determine their individual capabilities before diving the sites presented. Remember that water conditions can change within minutes at any time.

1

Overview of the Bay Islands

History

The Bay Islands, 40 miles off the northern coast of Honduras, erupted into life from volcanic action and coralline growth. The island's more recent history followed a similar blend of chaos and calm that included 400 years of conflict. Archaeological research strongly indicates that 600 years ago the Payan Indians inhabited the islands. The Payans, closely related to the Mayan Indians, developed extensive agricultural and trading enterprises. European visitation followed at later dates to disrupt Payan lifestyles. First to disembark were the Spanish, who claimed the islands for Spanish rule. Columbus, on his fourth voyage, sailed into Guanaja in 1502. He named the island "Isle of Pines" for its profusion of pine trees. Ship parts from this voyage still remain, encrusted in coral.

During the following years, unwary Payan Indians were captured as slaves and subsequently exported to work in Cuban mines. Those not captured fled the islands or died of imported diseases.

Agricultural production and increased exportation aroused the interest of other European countries. Dutch, French, and English ships set sail for the Bay Islands. Refugees, adventurers, and expatriates also found these islands well suited to their needs. Due to their strategic location, the islands became a popular pirate haven. The town of Savana Bight on Guanaja began by catering to pirates, and as late as the 1920s only the daring ventured into its harbor. Pirate raids everywhere were frequent. The remains of one such raid are still evident in Port Royal on Roatan. Port Royal was raided in 1792.

English persistence prevailed over others, straining English-Spanish relations regarding island rule. Continuous conflict was a way of life for many years. Individual villages were inhabited by either all English or all Spanish settlers.

Periodically, new English settlers populated the islands, establishing their agricultural operations. With them they brought several thousand slaves of Carib and African descent. The abolition of slavery found many of the freed slaves settling on Roatan.

4

Lush vegetation covers hillsides in a velvet green carpet. Islanders collect certain plants for use in herbal medicines. Photograph by K. Greenwood.

In the late 1800s, England ended years of conflict and ceded the Bay Islands to Honduran rule. The islands remain under the Honduran democratic rule today.

The years of intermittent English influence left their mark. Although the English language and culture predominate, Spanish culture and language are

Commercial fishing operations have been the primary industry for decades. Islanders process the catches for shipment in a packing house. Photograph by E. Klein.

slowly replacing English influences as more mainland Hondurans migrate to the islands for government positions, better employment, or island ways.

At this time the islands are economically stable. Commercial fishing fleets provide the mainstay of income. Tourism, in the form of divers and snorkelers, also provides income to the islands, although on a lesser scale than fishing.

The islands maintain their own distinctive cultural flavor, unspoiled by mass commercialism and mass tourism. Foreign influences are slow to change Bay Island lifestyles. Telephones and televisions are a rare sight.

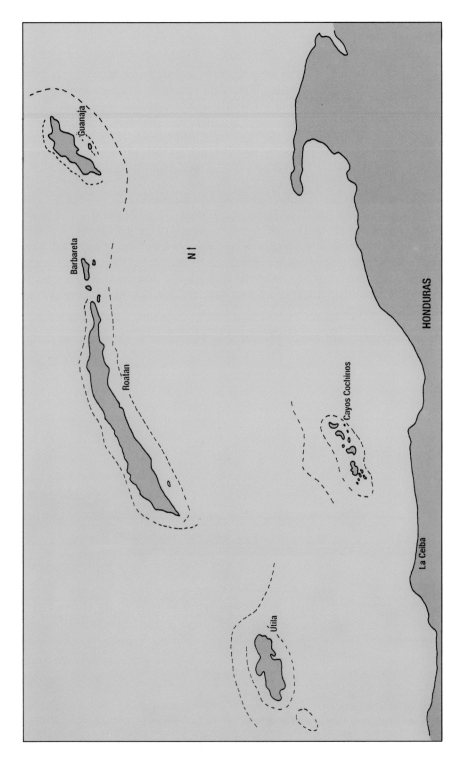

Guanaja

Barbareta

N

Roatán

Cayos Cochinos

HONDURAS

Útila

La Ceiba

The Islands

Despite turbulent times in the past, an excursion to the Bay Islands now is a trip of beauty and tranquility. The islands abound with lush tropical vegetation, spring-fed waters and waterfalls, and picturesque mountains. Each island is an individual in shape, geology, elevation, and water resources. Situated some 40 miles from the mainland, the islands form a chain that extends north-northeast. The Cayos Cochinos are the only islands not in the chain, and they are found between the mainland and Roatan.

Roatan. The largest of the islands, Roatan is approximately 36 green and mountainous miles long, and about a mile wide. Three major towns, Coxen Hole, French Harbor, and Oak Ridge contain most of the inhabitants. A paved road meanders most of the length of the island before turning to gravel. The newly built landing strip can accommodate jet aircraft landings. Unlike many Caribbean islands, but typical of the Bay Islands, Roatan boasts freshwater runoff from the mountains. Dive sites are located everywhere on the island's perimeter.

By paddle or motor, islanders go into town to do their marketing. Photograph by E. Klein.

Waterfalls scatter shimmering droplets as they tumble into clear cool pools.
Photograph by K. Greenwood.

Guanaja. Less elongated and deeper in width than Roatan, Guanaja's 9-mile length is sharply defined with steep verdant mountains. Waterfalls tumble melodically into clear, tranquil, and cool pools. Several cays encircle the island. The main settlement, on one such cay, is Bonacca. Approximately 4,000 people reside in Bonacca, and do so primarily because there are no sand flies. Other small villages on the island are Savana Bight and Mangrove Bight. No roads bisect Guanaja, so all travel around the island and associated cays is by boat. A small airport is serviced regularly by DC-3 aircraft arriving from LaCeiba or Roatan. Drinking water is delicious and obtained from spring-fed reservoirs. Several bands of coral reefs encircle the island, providing many good diving locations.

Barbareta. This island is relatively small and privately owned. Its mountains are unpopulated. A few locals, the resort owner's family, and resort staff usually live here year-round. One might believe that some areas of Barbareta have never been touched by man's hand. Travel is accomplished by boat or on foot. Supplies and visitors are brought over from Roatan or, on occasion, from Guanaja. Fresh water is readily available. Three miles of spectacular diving are minutes away from the shore. Close by, the Pigeon Cays offer excellent snorkeling and picnicking.

Utila. One of the smaller islands, Utila begins the chain of islands at the southwesternmost point. Large areas of flatland and extensive stretches of mature mangrove stands characterize this island. Here there is little surface water runoff, because most water quickly percolates through a porous limestone strata. A stream provides islanders with drinking water in addition to the rainwater collected by cisterns. A small airport allows access from the mainland, though flights are less frequent than to Roatan or Guanaja. Several reefs provide a variety of diving around the island.

Cayos Cochinos. Also referred to as the Hog Islands, this is a small group of tiny islands. The largest is Cochinos Grande. Several miles off the mainland coast, these islands are closer to the mainland than any other. The topography features rolling hills, a softening of the ruggedness apparent elsewhere. Cisterns collect rainwater. Available flights are few, therefore there are fewer visitors. The Cayos Cochinos are ideal for those seeking retreat and seclusion. Deep banks and shallow coral gardens are not far from any shore.

The total population of the Bay Islands, according to a 1988 census, was 21,550. The population is expected to double by early in the twenty-first century.

Getting There and Accommodations. Tan Sasha Airlines, American Airlines, Taca Airlines, and Pan American Airlines transport visitors to the Honduran mainland from Houston, New Orleans, and Miami. Daily flights to most of the islands are provided by Air Islena. Although reservations may be booked in the U.S.A., Air Islena tickets must be purchased only in Honduras.

Tan Sasha Airlines delivers eager passengers to Honduran resorts. Photograph by M. Patoka.

Each of the Bay Islands has resorts, guest houses, and/or small hotels to accommodate the diving enthusiast.

Customs and Immigration. A valid passport is necessary to enter Honduras. A return ticket is required. Tourist visas are obtained en route. Visitors may remain in Honduras for up to 6 months. Monthly renewal of the visa during the 6-month period is obtained in each island's immigration office.

Currency. The currency of the Honduras Bay Islands is the lempira. U.S. dollars are accepted at most resort operations. The official exchange rate is currently approximately 5 lempiras for $1 U.S. Credit card acceptance is variable; cards are not always recognized, though they are honored at most diving establishments.

2

Coral Reefs and Marine Life

The coral reef is a world beneath tropical seas, and what a world! A rainbow of color assaults your eyes; formations of all sizes rise, ever-growing from sandy bottoms. At first glance, the coral reef may seem to be a simple cluster of rocks or solid wall, but this is not the case at all. It is instead a highly complex, stratified ecosystem. Tropical rain forests are the closest terrestrial counterpart. Both reef and rain forest are dependent upon sunlight. Sun filters through the strata, and at each level you'll find particular organisms whose needs match available light, shelter, and food.

Throughout the years, two different theories have been introduced to explain coral reef origins. The first theory was developed by Charles Darwin, who thought that three geomorphological reef types were formed by

Orange coral polyps stretch delicate tentacles in an exuberant display. Photograph by J. Ford.

varying degrees of land subsidence. The three types are *fringing reefs,* or coral masses extending waterward from the shore; *barrier reefs,* formed when the land mass partially subsided and the reef was separated from the land; and *atolls,* created when the land mass completely submerged. Atolls are commonly found throughout the Pacific.

Reginald Daly hypothesized that reefs were formed by glacial actions. His theory, known as the glacial control theory, suggests that during glacial periods in the earth's history, water levels fell and the corals were killed by the colder temperatures. Glacial surf mercilessly beat away the shores, cutting platforms into the rock. When the climate warmed, water levels rose, and the edges of the platforms developed rapid growth of coral, producing barrier reefs and atolls.

Research evidence indicates that both theories are correct. Reefs may have been developed by either of these theories or a combination of both theories.

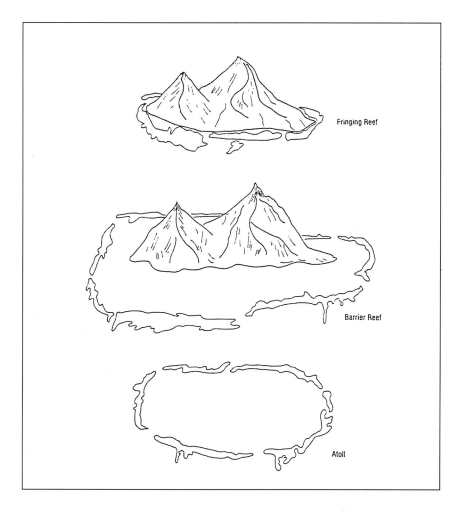

Fringing Reef

Barrier Reef

Atoll

But what is a coral reef? Corals are animals. Coral reefs are based upon thousands of individual coral animals called polyps. These polyps form immense colonies. Each coral polyp continually secretes calcium carbonate. The polyp is pushed up as it builds and its calcium carbonate secretions harden. It then remains on the surface of the skeleton it has created. This process is continuous. Thousands of years must pass before the towering formations and beautiful coral gardens project their splendor. Research has indicated that the coral growth would not be possible without one essential factor: zooxanthellae. Zooxanthellae are dinoflagellate algae that live within the coral polyp and are required for the calcification process.

The bottom of the coral polyp is attached to its structure, but the top is composed of small tentacles that move continually, collecting minute zooplankton to provide the coral animal with food. To the casual observer these tentacles appear to be tiny flowers, but if the diver looks closely, each individual tentacle can be seen waving gently in the current.

Hard corals usually feed at night, extending flowerlike tentacles to catch plankton drifting by. Photograph by J. Ford.

There are two types of coral, hard and soft. Coral type is totally dependent upon the skeleton that is secreted. Hard corals comprise the backbone of the coral reef. These corals deposit a solid wall of calcium carbonate that forms the hard rock-like structures. Soft corals have only microscopically thin spicules of calcium carbonate deposited in their structure, similar to intricate webs. The soft corals, lacking rigid support, gracefully move to and fro with the current. They are often mistaken for plants decorated with tiny, delicately colored flowers. Except for the towering stands of pillar coral, hard corals generally extend their tentacles at night, whereas soft corals feed by day.

In Caribbean locations where the winds blow constantly a well-marked windward reef front is usually found. The reef front is characterized by a healthy coral development of spurs or fingers that jut seaward. These fingers are angled perpendicularly to the shore, yielding rows of ridges interspersed with sand canyons. The formations provide a means for waves to dissipate their energy. Waves surge up through the canyons and then wash back carrying loads of particulate matter. Behind the reef front is the wind-

A trunkfish greets a visitor in the shallows.

ward reef crest. Here, a mixture of hard and soft corals abound, but elkhorn corals predominate. Inside the crest begins the lagoon. The lagoon is a more tranquil place, where seahorses can wrap their caudal fins around seagrasses without fear of strong surges carrying them away. It is an area of smaller patches of soft corals and hard corals intermixed with seagrasses and bottom-dwelling fish and organisms. Lagoon depths in the Caribbean usually range from 5 to 15 meters.

Each reef zone possesses distinctive animal populations and characteristics. These same distinctions make each coral reef unique. Island topography, wind action, wave action, and water depths may all play a part in altering each reef's characteristics.

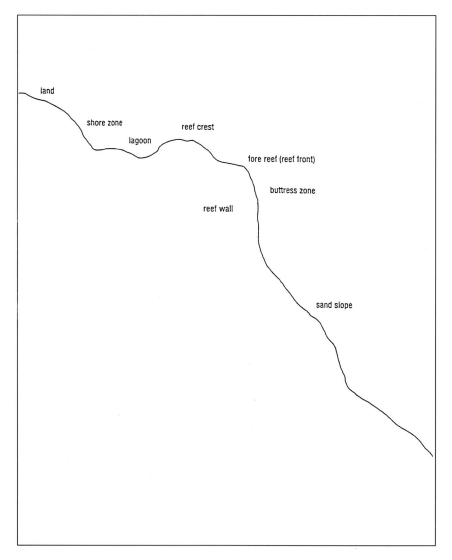

Conservation of the Reefs

The complex interrelationships between reefs and their inhabitants are part of a worldwide process which began millions of years ago. The magnitude of the reef structure is almost inconceivable. Perhaps only a tropical rain forest can parallel a reef for abundance and diversity of life.

And, like the rain forest, the reef is a fragile environment. Coral reefs survive in a very limited range of tolerance. Corals optimally survive in nutrient-poor, clear, warm waters. One might think that in such nutrient-poor waters there would be few living organisms. However, biological productivity is high. This may be partly due to several factors: the clarity of the water allows substantial sunlight penetration, stable warm temperature conditions, an efficient recycling of the nutrients that are present, and a symbiotic relationship between coral and zooxanthellae. Organisms, from the lowest one-celled to the most complex, interact, reproduce, find nursery grounds, feed, and find shelter within the reef environs.

The reef is not only important to its inhabitants, but to mankind for food on the table or for the new discoveries in medical research that may save lives. In varying degrees, however, man has impacted the coral reef ecosystems, stressing the limited tolerances throughout the world. Increase in population, demand for food, and tourism have all directly or indirectly altered the reefs. Sedimentation associated with deforestation, road building, and channel dredging for boat passage has smothered coral polyps. In man's

The author maintains neutral buoyancy while drifting along a reef. Photograph by K. Greenwood.

search for seafood some of the reefs have been exploited to the extent that dynamite has been used for easier catches. Raw sewage and other pollutants increase nutrient-loading, causing the biological nature to change and leading to the subsequent death of the reef.

Divers also, even unintentionally, may cause severe damage to the reefs by grabbing, poking, breaking, and kicking the corals. Touching a coral injures its tissues, thus subjecting the corals to invasion and infection. Poor buoyancy control causes divers to bump into coral and results in damage. Barren patches in the coral wall give evidence of such damage.

Various studies have indicated that improper buoyancy control is a major cause of physical damage to the reef, and that the use of gloves allows divers to touch what an ungloved hand might not have touched.

Worldwide efforts have been initiated to curb the deterioration of coral reefs. Educational courses are offered regarding the effects of pollution, sedimentation, and overfishing. Fisheries management has taken hold in some areas.

How can a diver work to conserve this valuable resource and his or her favorite playground? Divers can: (1) try to maintain neutral buoyancy at all times so that they don't bounce off the corals, (2) touch with eyes only, (3) eliminate the use of gloves, (4) refrain from collecting live shells and corals, (5) pass on the knowledge learned to those divers who have never experienced the fragility of life on a coral reef, and lastly, (6) avoid tossing plastic materials into the sea. Plastic items are swallowed by fish, turtles, and birds, causing their deaths.

Each and every one of us has a responsibility to conserve and protect our reefs. With increased numbers of divers, all must now be continually aware of how easily the dive site can be spoiled for the diver's own next expedition.

The reefs are alive! Photograph by J. Ford.

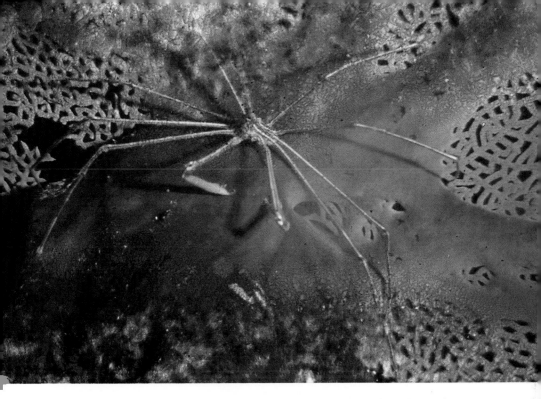

The coral reef is a natural habitat for brilliantly colored animals of all species, such as this arrow crab on a gorgonian. Photograph by J. Ford.

Marine Life of the Bay Islands

The reefs are a natural habitat for the brilliantly colored tropical fish and invertebrates found there in such large numbers. Coral reefs are a flamboyant display of life. Each animal, coral, fish, tunicate, or lobster plays a vital role in ensuring that the reef maintains a high level of productivity. As with all life, each animal has developed adaptations designed for its survival. It is only due to the emergence of scuba diving in recent years that biologists have been able to begin studying the habits of marine life in the reef ecosystem.

Fish and invertebrates alike feed upon a variety of food sources, at times and within territories delicately adjusted for their survival in a very crowded habitat. Reproduction strategies are just as selectively complex. Coloration varies from the drab to the brilliant. Colors are often used as a means of camouflage. In fish, having extra "eyes" or stripes to blend in with background habitat are typical examples of such camouflage.

Most of the animals living on the reefs, including the corals, are invertebrates. Invertebrate animals are those that do not have a backbone in their bodies. These animals are widely dissimilar in structure, however. Some are primitive in composition while others are extremely complex.

Fish. Ichthyologists have identified approximately 21,500 different fish species worldwide, and 30–40% of the total species diversity may be found on tropical reefs alone. A good representation of these swim gracefully in Bay Island waters. It is not unusual, under close investigation, to see at least 50 individual species living harmoniously around a single coral head, in an area no larger than the average kitchen table. Some of the fish species have been briefly described throughout the text. Each is different; each has individual characteristics.

Several species of coral compete for space in this area of the reef.

Corals. These animals form immense colonies. By continually secreting calcium carbonate they create formations of amazing beauty. Many of the corals have brilliant coloring while others are tinted with shades of brown. The coral's mouth is ringed with flowerlike tentacles. Each tentacle has stinging nematocysts, characteristic of the Cnidaria phylum. Corals may be found anywhere there are warm tropical seas, clear water, and stable nutrient levels. Each species lives in a different zone of the reef and with varying levels of sunlight penetration. A few are described throughout this guide.

Each sponge's skeleton is punctuated with millions of tiny pores. Photograph by J. Ford.

Sponges. Sponges play an important part in reef ecology. Their shape and growth vary widely and are dependent upon available space, nature of the substrate, and water flow. Some, like the loggerhead sponge, may be enormous, while others may be minute. Sponges are all sessile, which means they are permanently attached and unable to move about. Many species are present in the Bay Islands and are mentioned in the text.

Anemones and Nudibranchs. Anemones are solitary creatures. They are attractive animals with brightly colored tentacles of green, blue, orange, red, purple, white, or pink. Stinging nematocysts arm the tentacles. Many anemones provide a home and protection to small shrimp, crabs, or fish. Spiral or ringed anemones host pistol shrimp, which in turn clean off any necrotic tissue on the anemones. Another commonly found anemone is the pink-tipped anemone.

Great Caribbean anemones are scattered throughout the reefs. Photograph by J. Ford.

Nudibranchs belong to the Mollusca (shellfish) phylum. They are gorgeous, tiny marine animals, whose bodies have numerous cerata, or frilly skin, on the dorsal area. Nudibranch bodies are highly decorative and brilliantly colored. Occasionally they float freely, but most of the time they are found slowly creeping along something solid. Several species inhabit the Bay Island reefs.

One of the problems in describing marine life is determining which hundreds of species to exclude and which few to include. Therefore, only some of the more commonly observed or interesting species are discussed in the text. Please note that there are literally hundreds of marine fish and invertebrate species to be found in the Bay Islands, as elsewhere in the Caribbean.

Night Diving in the Bay Islands

A night dive can be an exciting conclusion to a day's diving. Many of the animals that rest hidden or curled up by day come out at night. Basket starfish, which would be unnoticed by day, unfurl their network of arms in a truly magnificent display. Parrotfish secrete a mucous cocoon for protection and can be observed placidly sleeping within. Crabs, lobster, and shrimp begin foraging. An octopus may erupt from a dark recess in the coral. Sea cucumbers stretch into long tubes. Squirrelfish become busy. These are but a few animals to watch for during a night dive.

Night diving is not difficult. Divers should plan ahead, prepare their gear during the day, and place lights both on the boat and below the boat for reference. If diving from shore, establish a light on shore for the return. The best depths for marine life sightings at night are shallow. Moonless nights are best for the greatest numbers of animals to appear. If a diver stays close to the boat and reef and uses safety precautions, a memorable dive is there for the taking.

Octopi are a common sight on most night dives. Photograph by M. Patoka.

Hazardous Marine Life

Most marine animals are defensive, not aggressive, by nature. Marine animals primarily become dangerous when scared or threatened in some manner. Injuries, of course, may occur when a diver inadvertently comes into contact with a toxin-filled spine, tentacle, or bristle. In many cases, if a diver or snorkeler watches where he places his body, no harm will come from any of the species listed below. However, because there is always a potential for accidents and injuries, several animals are described that require careful attention.

Barracuda are attracted to glitter and waving fingers that might look like fish.

Barracuda (Family Sphyraendidae). Barracuda have an unearned name for ferociousness. Perhaps it is due to a full mouth of jagged teeth and the curiosity that lures the barracuda to follow divers; however, attacks are extremely rare. The barracuda's eyesight is poor, and moving fingers may appear to be small fish to them. A barracuda is also attracted to glitter, so if one of these fish is known to be in the area, avoid wearing jewelry and avoid waving your fingers around. Respect its power and speed. Barracuda bodies are elongated and silvery with dark oblique bars on the upper portion. A mature adult may be six feet long.

The tiny bristleworm can leave a painful impression if touched. Photograph by J. Ford.

Bristleworms (*Hermodice carunculata*). These tiny creatures inflict a very painful and extremely toxic sting when touched. They are found crawling over rocks, in seagrass beds, and on coral heads. This green or red ten-inch-long worm has bristles that "tuft" up, break off, and embed themselves in a diver's skin and/or gloves when touched. To avoid contact, be sure to look before touching anything.

Fire Coral (Class Hydrozoa, *Millepora alicornis*). Fire corals are not true corals. They are polyps that attach to other structures forming brown and white solid lumps, large encrusting surfaces, or strongly branched config-urations. They possess powerful stinging cells called nematocysts. When touched, the stinging cells eject the toxic threads from within. Contact with a fire coral results in an immediate unpleasant burning sensation.

Fire corals grow splendidly in shallow waters.

Jellyfish (Classes Scyphozoa and Hydrozoa). There are several species of jellyfish and siphonophores that contain stinging nematocysts in their tentacles. Jellyfish swim slowly in a pulsating motion near the surface or at mid-depths. Most are bell-shaped and nearly transparent. If they are observed in heavy concentrations, do not enter the water, but move on to another area. If in the water, avoid contact by simply swimming away. Contact, dependent upon the species, may result in reactions from a slight burning sensation to extreme pain.

A moray eel resides in small caves and attacks only when threatened. Photograph by J. Ford.

Moray Eels (Family Muraenidae). Moray eels are classified with fishes, although they are often mistaken for members of the snake family. They are fleshy, elongated, snakelike fish. Their mouths open and close constantly for respiration purposes. A secretive creature that forages at night, its eyesight is poor. Divers are usually bitten only when reaching into a crevice that is the home of a moray, thus threatening its safety. If bitten, a diver should remain calm and keep still. Once the moray recognizes that your finger is not a fish, it will release its hold.

Rays (Family Dasyatididae and Myliobatidae). Rays also belong to the fish group, but they have cartilage for a skeleton rather than bone. Bodies are butterfly-diamond shaped. Many have a barbed spine on the "tail." Coloration varies. Stingrays normally spend their time buried in the sand, and are only dangerous when stepped on because the ray will whip its tail up in defense. The barbed spine in contact with a diver or snorkeler's skin is painful and may cause swelling.

25

Notice that the scorpionfish blends in perfectly with its background. Photograph by M. Patoka.

Scorpionfish (Family Scorpaenidae). If you see a mottled "rock" with eyes, you have probably found a scorpionfish. All coloration is expertly blended with the substrate below. The scorpionfish possesses toxin in its dorsal fins, which may be painful upon contact. Use caution when placing fingers. Always look first.

Sea urchins inhabit recesses in the coralline formations. Photograph by M. Patoka.

Sea Urchins (Class Echinoidea). The long-spined sea urchin (*Diadema antillarum*) is an animal that looks like a large, round pincushion. These "pins" or spines are what inflict pain on a diver who roughly handles or steps on the urchin. The spines can break off easily and penetrate the skin. The animals are generally found in shallow waters in coral flats, seagrass beds, or niches in the coral.

A nurse shark peacefully sleeps under a ledge. Photograph by M. Patoka.

Sharks (Class Chondrichthyes, order Squaliformes). Numerous species of sharks inhabit the tropical waters of the Caribbean. As with rays, a cartilaginous skeleton replaces the bony skeleton found in other fish. Sharks give live birth. All are carnivores and unpredictable in varying degrees. Many may be dangerous. Some may not exhibit aggressive behavior unless provoked, while others may attack at will. No attempt should be made to play with any shark, "sleeping" or not. There have been no reported shark attacks in the Bay Islands to the author's knowledge.

3

Diving in the Bay Islands

Thousand-foot walls festooned with deepwater lace, coral gardens towering with enormous monuments of pillar coral, 60-foot-deep ledges crowded with blackcap basslets, mini-walls clustered with bluebell tunicates, pinnacles overgrown with azure vase sponges, and shy indigo hamlets peering from niches are all characteristic of Bay Island diving. Typical in the Caribbean? No, many marine species are plentiful in the Bay Islands where elsewhere their variety has disappeared or is severely diminished. Large groupers and moray eels are a common sight. On any given dive it would not be unusual to see a loggerhead turtle or spotted eagle ray gracefully gliding by.

Each of the Bay Islands offers memorable diving. The reefs are so extensive that it would take months of daily diving to see each known segment.

It would be unrealistic, therefore, to try to enumerate all the sites within the confines of any one book. On the following pages a number of the more popular and interesting locations are described, island by island.

The reader may assume that for each site presented there are others in proximity similar in nature.

Weather and Water Conditions

The weather in the Bay Islands is virtually idyllic year round. Air temperatures are pleasantly mild, rarely rising above 90°F or dropping below 75°F. A mild to moderate easterly breeze caresses the reefs and islands on most days.

Climatic changes may occur for several days at a time during the winter, when storms from the north may bring heavier seas and rain. Although rare, hurricanes are also a possibility during the summer and fall months.

Water temperatures normally vary only a few degrees. In the winter, temperatures may drop to 78°F and then rise to 82°F in the summer.

Water current conditions may fluctuate but on the whole currents are slight. High tide to low tide is approximately a twelve-inch difference.

The leeward and windward reefs differ in water visibility periodically, but for the most part visibility often exceeds 150 feet. Clarity increases the farther from shore one dives.

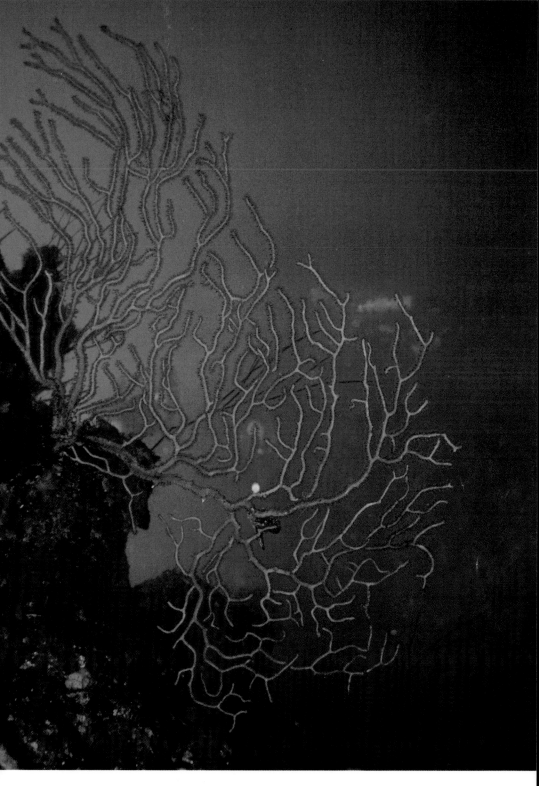

Elegant deepwater lace grows in splendor along thousand-foot walls.

4

Diving in Roatan

Roatan is sandwiched between the 30 miles of dynamic reefs along its northern and southern coasts. The north side entices the diver to explore robust fringing/barrier reefs that explode with color and exhilarate with breathtaking views. These drop-offs feature a wild profusion of exotic aquatic life. On the south side the reefs are closer to shore: fringing reefs that are less than a quarter mile from land. The fairy-tale vista awaiting one to the south is more delicate than the offshore reefs to the north.

Both coasts offer 30 miles of superb spur/canyon configurations, coral gardens, ledges, overhangs, and vertical fissures. Miles of reef have yet to be explored by visitors. Azure vase sponges, black crinoids, black coral, deepwater lace, pillar corals, hawksbill turtles, and other stunning marine life grace the reefs. Several wrecks have been documented throughout the area for wreck-diving enthusiasts. The dive sites that typify diving in Roatan are Mary's Place, Prince Albert Wreck, Doc's Dive, The Enchanted Forest, West End Wall, West Bay sites, and the Halfmoon Bay sites.

Iridescent tube sponges compete for space among the profusion of soft corals.

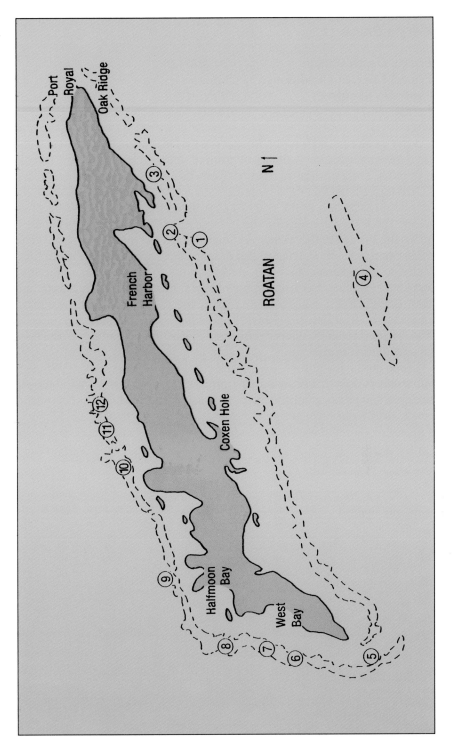

Typical Depth Range:	20–100 feet
Typical Current Conditions:	Minimal
Expertise Required:	Intermediate
Access:	Boat

Mary's Place is THE dive on Roatan's reefs. One cannot go to Roatan without exploring this superb site. As a result of volcanic activity, Mary's Place resembles a thumb-like projection from the wall. Two sheer faults are carved through the thumb. A mooring buoy is positioned over an area of 20-foot depth at the top of the reef. To start this different and beautiful dive, one descends the mooring line and swims east to the wall. Once on the wall, turn right, locate the sheer canyon (fissure), enter, and slowly progress. The fissure starts at a 20-foot depth and drops to 70 feet at its deepest. Another fault line soon comes into focus at right angles to the first. This fault bottoms out at 60 feet, but rises only to 40 feet. Enter the second fissure and swim through to the wall, then turn right again, hugging the wall, swimming until once again at the opposite end of the first fissure and enter it at the west side. Swim through to the point of entry of the fault and return to the boat on a reciprocal course.

Inside the faults, at forty feet, black coral grows in profusion, although the numbers may have dwindled from illegal harvesting. Many copper sweepers and groupers inhabit the area. Outside on the wall a number of hard corals, deepwater lace, and fish species may be identified.

Silversides part to allow a diver's passage through a fissure at Mary's Place. Photograph by M. Patoka.

Prince Albert Wreck 2

Typical Depth:	35–85 feet
Typical Current Conditions:	Variable
Expertise Required:	Intermediate
Access:	From shore or boat

An interesting wreck to explore, the *Prince Albert* was an island freighter that sank sometime in 1987. Several years' growth now covers the 140-foot hull. A collection of fish species have found suitable homes in the cave-like structure. The wreck lies in the channel on the southeast side of Roatan. She is situated in the western side of the channel entry point, and close to the fringing reef. Sunk in an upright position, she rests in 85 feet of water on a sloping white sandy bottom. A mooring buoy is present. From the mooring buoy one should swim a few yards to the south to find her. Visibility ranges from mediocre to excellent, depending upon the state of the tide. No lights are required to enter the wreck and penetration is possible through most portals.

Thousands of silversides hover inside. Wrasses and other bottom dwelling fish will be observed here. If one looks closely, spiny oysters may also be observed. Algae growth and soft corals protrude from the hull structure. Silversides drift together in large schools, forming a shimmering synchronized display for the watcher.

Near the wreck lives a colony of garden eels. A bonus in the vicinity is a DC-3 airplane to inspect.

A profusion of colorful corals and sponges grow in jumbled array throughout Roatan's reefs. Photograph by M. Patoka.

33

Typical Depth Range:	30–120 feet
Typical Current Conditions:	Minimal
Expertise Required:	Novice
Access:	Boat

Doc's Dive can best be described as a delightful mini-wall consisting of varying coral formations, mini-caves, canyons, and overhangs. It is one of several sites located east of French Harbor and within the landward side of the fringing reef. During heavy seas (even during calm seas) this is a perfect spot for a remarkable dive. A mooring buoy is present. The top of the reef begins in 30 feet of water and drops down to approximately 110–120 feet. Upon descent from the mooring line, drift out to the wall and veer left, keep-

Goatfish scour the sandy bottom using their chin barbels to detect tiny critters. Photograph by K. Greenwood.

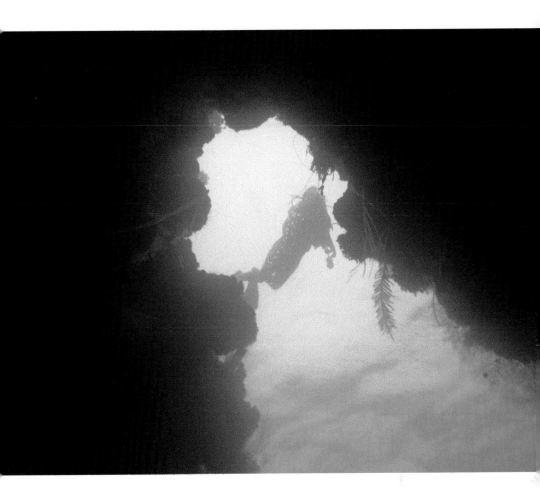

A diver hovers outside the entrance of a cave. Photograph by M. Patoka.

ing the wall to your left. Fingerlike valleys indent the wall. Soft corals sway in harmony with the current. Sea turtles and spotted eagle rays are a common sight. Anemones wait for prey to become entangled in their tentacles.

If you choose to veer right at the wall, however, another view awaits. To the right, not far from the wall entry point, is a kidney-shaped opening. Entering the opening, you will find yourself in a small cave illuminated by two shafts of light. Exploring the cave, one might find crabs, lobsters, and other marine life that prefers the quiet darkness.

Along the wall are numerous angelfish, butterflyfish, wrasses, triggerfish, trumpetfish, parrotfish, groupers, and damsels. This is a terrific location for those interested in snorkeling adventure as well as experienced and novice divers who desire a site close to shore that is full of marine life.

Bay Island commercial lobstermen spend months at sea in search of the spiny lobster. Photograph by B. Chambers.

Angelfish

The darlings of the underwater reef community, angelfish belong to the family Pomacanthidae. These strikingly beautiful and curious fish may be found near caves and sheltered areas anywhere. In general, angelfish have laterally flattened bodies to maintain swimming speed. Angelfish consume sponges for their main diet, supplemented with algae, tunicates, and anemones. If possible, juveniles have even more striking coloration than the adults. Queen angels are so named for the regally painted crown on their foreheads. They are brilliant blue and green, with yellow caudal fins. French angels are gray with gold flecks on the body scales, and often swim in pairs. Juveniles are a distinctive black and yellow. There are several other species of angelfish found throughout the Caribbean.

Typical Depth Range:	55 feet to unlimited
Typical Current Conditions:	Variable
Expertise Required:	Intermediate, with divemaster
Access:	Boat

The Enchanted Forest is a recently discovered paradise dive! It is located a distance offshore from French Harbor. Its sheer plunging wall is exquisite and pristine.

Angelfish are the darlings of the Caribbean waters. They can be found near coral heads in seagrass beds and also on offshore reefs. Photograph by K. Greenwood.▶

Deepwater Lace is a delicate brown or black coral that looks red when photographed in artificial light. Photograph by M. Patoka.▼

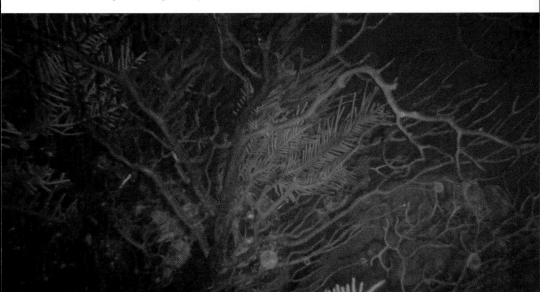

The top of the reef is in deep water, starting at the 55- to 60-foot depth. From the top of the reef the wall drops literally into the abyss: the Bartlett Trench, in excess of 5,000 feet deep. At the reef crest, ridge after ridge is punctuated with huge forests of staghorn and pillar corals. On the forereef enormous boulder corals form shingled overhangs and ledges. Black coral and azure vase sponges grow in profusion. There is nothing like gliding by a black coral forest to stimulate excitement. Deepwater lace adds character and beauty to an already fabulous cliff structure.

As you might expect, the marine life here is that usually associated with deeper offshore waters. Sea turtles grace the scenery. Black crinoids sit atop large barrel sponges. Queen and ocean triggerfish, scrawled filefish, schools of jacks, tobaccofish, hogfish, blackcap basslets, and black durgeons are abundant. Scrawled filefish are an interesting breed. When threatened they hide in crevices and niches by triggering their modified dorsal fin to lock it into place in an erect position. Sailors of the past are said to have dried the skin for use to strike matches. The scrawled filefish are slender, with bodies decorated with blue scrawls and blotches, and black spots.

The scrawled filefish is a sleek and beautifully decorated species that prefers deeper water such as the Enchanted Forest. Photograph by K. Greenwood.

This is a dive that will never be forgotten. Please keep in mind at all times, however, that it is a deep dive; careful monitoring of buoyancy, air consumption, and gauges is a *must*.

Typical Depth Range:	15–120 feet
Typical Current Conditions:	Variable
Expertise Required:	Novice, with divemaster
Access:	Boat

West End Wall is located, as expected, off the western tip of Roatan. It is actually two popular dive sites, one shallower than the other, featuring two separate zones of reef. The shallower site is located closer to shore and begins its sharp descent in 15 feet of water, then drops to 120 feet. Farther out in the open water, the deeper site has a reef crest at 30–40-foot depth, which then gradually slopes seaward to more than one hundred feet. Both sites have a mooring buoy from which one would descend to swim several yards to the wall. *A cautionary note:* As there is generally a strong current present at these sites, the diver should always begin the dive against the current.

It's hard to imagine that this delightful garden of coral is actually many animal colonies.

Flamingo tongues slowly nibble on the soft corals they inhabit. Photograph by J. Ford.

The deeper reef displays a flatter profile than the shallower reef. Here are found numerous schools of pelagic fish, large groupers, turtles, and even the occasional shark.

The shallower reef, like the deeper site, exhibits prolific marine life. Fish of many species flit in and out of the coral formations. Soft corals move gracefully in the slow dance of the currents. Gorgonians are one of the soft corals found everywhere. They are important to the ecosystem of the reef. Other animals such as flamingo tongues, tunicates, and small gobies find food and shelter in seafan latticework. Whether the diver is impressed by the more pelagic marine life or the shallower reef critters, these sites will offer it all.

Eel Garden 6

Typical Depth Range:	15–100 feet
Typical Current Conditions:	Minimal
Expertise Required:	Novice
Access:	Boat

The Eel Garden offers more than the usual sheer drop-offs found elsewhere. Located just off West Bay, this site is a relatively shallow reef that gently slopes seaward. When visualizing it, think of a novice ski slope with many sand patches. If you think sand patches are barren land, think again! It is here that colonies of garden eels reside, in company with sailfin blennies, rays, lizardfish, goatfish, and flounders.

A mooring buoy is present. The top of the reef is a mere 15 feet from the surface. From there the reef slopes down to 100 feet. The reef does continue onto a wall that drops still farther. Interest on this dive, however, is focused upon the sand flats at the 50-foot level. Colonies of garden eels are found here. Row upon row of the shy eels poke their bodies out from their sandy holes. To observe these shy creatures, a diver must approach slowly. If the approach threatens the eels they will retreat in waves, leaving nothing but a vista of sand. To catch an eel in the camera's shutter may be a most frustrating effort, but patience should reward the photographer with a rare shot.

A bar jack scans an area that is usually alive with swaying eels. Photograph by K. Greenwood.

Sunshine damsels vigorously defend their territories, which can be identified by noticeable patches of algal growth.

In addition to this splendid display, there are coral outcroppings and crevices to view. Myriad shallow reef fish are present. It would be unusual not to see an abundance of angelfish, butterflyfish, damselfish, hamlets and red spotted hawkfish. Note that wherever a damselfish has outlined her territory, patches of algae grow in profusion. Damsels are pugnacious fish, afraid of nothing in defense of territory or eggs. Don't be surprised to come face to face with one species or another if invading their territory.

Typical Depth Range: 5–50 feet
Typical Current Conditions: Minimal
Expertise Required: Novice
Access: Boat

It's a feeding frenzy at Herbie's Fantasy! This is a spectacular shallow dive. A diver can either watch or help feed the many species of grouper or the resident green or spotted moray eels.

Located just off the West Bay on the main reef chain, there is very little surge or current, making it a great site for both diver and snorkeler. The reef crest is just a few feet below the water's surface. The mooring buoy is situated close to the sand canyon where all the action begins. A wall gradually slopes to 50 feet. An adjacent sand canyon bottoms out at 30 feet. The sand canyon is filled with little caverns and boulder coral, which provide ledges sheltering fish and invertebrates. Proceeding from the mooring buoy, a diver would swim along the wall to the left to the sand canyon several fin kicks away. Be prepared to greet the resident groupers and morays who are patiently waiting for handouts in the sand canyon. Divemasters often bring sardines to appease the grouper appetites.

At Herbie's Fantasy one can find impressive forests of elkhorn and staghorn corals. Photograph by B. Chambers.

Closer to the surface are superb forests of magnificent elkhorn and staghorn coral. Note that these species of coral are dominant and few other coral species co-exist in this area. Farther down are brilliant azure vases, characteristic of Bay Island diving. Shallow reef fish and other critters are plentiful. A host of blue tangs, snappers, butterflyfish, parrotfish, blue chromis, grunts, and damsels pick at the small crustaceans, algae, and corals. Roaming around, one might spot a flamboyant nudibranch or flamingo tongue. Parrotfish are a principal source of sand on the reefs, using their parrot-like beaks to break apart coral in search of algae. The crunching noise a diver may notice is probably a parrotfish. Coloration is vivid and varies from species to species. They are common on most reefs.

Listen a moment; the sound emanating from the reef is probably a parrotfish picking at the coral. Photograph by J. Ford.

Typical Depth Range:	15–150 feet
Typical Current Conditions:	Minimal
Expertise Required:	Novice
Access:	Boat

Lighthouse Reef is a popular dive for the novice diver and snorkeler alike. It is positioned near Half Moon Bay, across from the lighthouse on the north (leeward) side of the island. Shallow diving with emphasis on a full panoply of marine activity is in order here.

A mooring buoy is established on the edge of a sandy bowl cradled in the middle of the reef crest. The top of the reef here is 15 feet deep. The base of the sand arena is 25 feet. Encircling the sand is a coralline wreath decorated with soft and hard corals. Sea feathers are one of the soft corals found that add a distinctive terrestrial forest atmosphere to the arena walls. In the chinks of some coralline growth one might find a file clam or lima spreading its tentacles outward from a flame-colored body cavity.

In a symbiotic relationship, the Pederson cleaning shrimp lives within the shelter of an anemone's tentacles. Photograph by J. Ford.

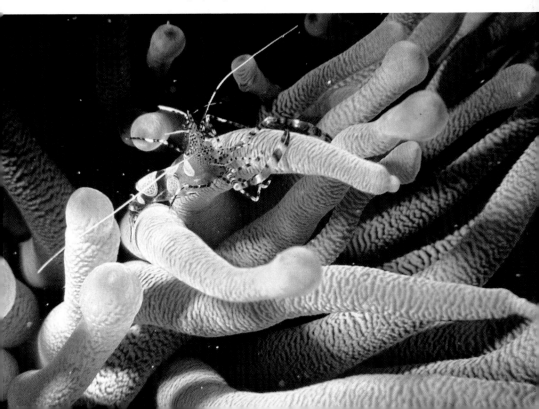

A look into a tube sponge might show any number of crabs, gobies, or starfish.

Leaving the sand patch and continuing on a few feet, the diver will reach the reef wall. The wall drops to 150 feet. Typical ridges and sand canyons have formed at this reef. Because there is virtually no current or surge, a diver may proceed along the wall in either direction.

Marine life is varied. There are crevices, sandy patches, coral gardens, and ledges where a host of fish and invertebrates live. Arrow crabs and spiral anemones live under cracks or rocks. Pistol shrimp, in a symbiotic relationship, live within the tangle of the spiral anemone's tentacles. Sea fans, hamlets, lizardfish, wrasses, angelfish, porcupinefish, harlequin bass, and many others share this environment. Harlequin bass are another small relative of the groupers, possessing the same general physical attributes except size. To the sharp eye this species can commonly be seen at least once on a given dive. Harlequins are bottom dwellers, preferring sandy patches. Wildly patterned with brown blotches, they have vertical black bands and a white ventral area.

Typical Depth Range:	15–500 feet
Typical Current Conditions:	Minimal
Expertise Required:	Advanced
Access:	Boat

Hole in the Wall is an exceptional deep dive for the advanced diver, and an experience to cherish. Located east of Lighthouse Reef, it is near Half Moon Bay on the north side of the island.

A mooring buoy is present. Beneath the buoy the reef crest commences at a depth of 15 feet. To reach the Hole, descend the mooring line, veer right, and follow the crevicelike canyon to the Hole. Leaving the Hole, you may either follow a reciprocal course or continue around the canyon to a series of small caverns at the canyon's mouth. After visiting the caverns, simply cut across the canyon mouth back to the mooring line. You might consider snorkeling over the canyon rim to the Hole to conserve air and bottom time. As you hover at the rim of the Hole, you will notice that the Hole resembles a large funnel. The mouth of the funnel narrows into a tube with only a 25-foot span and reaches depths of 400–500 feet. The caverns are a won-

The ridge and canyon configuration is typical of Bay Island reefs. Photograph by M. Patoka.

derful spot to investigate niches and crevices that could contain any variety of nocturnal marine life.

Although there is not an abundance of marine life at the Hole, there are large branches of black coral to gaze upon. Deep pelagic species may be encountered. Near the reef crest the life becomes more profuse. Stands of hard and soft corals occupy the region, accompanied by shallow water fish species.

For the advanced diver this is truly a terrific dive. Remember, however, that it is a deep dive; careful monitoring of the gauges and bottom time should be maintained.

A queen angelfish poses warily for the photographer. Photograph by J. Ford.

Typical Depth Range:	15–100 feet
Typical Current Conditions:	Minimal
Expertise Required:	Novice
Access:	Boat

Pillar Coral Point is aptly named for the profusion of pillar coral that majestically rises from the reef wall. Located close to Half Moon Bay on the leeward side of the island, a gently sloping reef initiates its descent from 15 feet of water and winds its way down to more than 100 feet. A mooring buoy prevents anchor damage to the coral. The abundance of pillar coral is the focus of the dive and these grow particularly well at the 30–40-foot level. In this shallow water region, the forest of pillar coral is outstanding. An easy dive, you simply descend the mooring line, drift out to the wall seconds away, and descend another 15–20 feet.

The wall itself is built with impressive ridges, coral overhangs, and small cavities. Exploration of its secrets is an experience in delightful anticipation. Luxurious coral gardens compete with the pillar coral. Juvenile spotted drums hide under ledges. Fairy basslets orient their bodies toward the light sand patches or sunlight. Queen triggerfish float by in regal stature. One of the most exciting and graceful fish to catch your eye, the queen triggerfish is decorated a blue-green with brilliant blue rays radiating from its eyes and extending from snout to pectoral fins. They are named for a "trigger" device, a modified dorsal fin that can lock into an erect position enabling them to hide motionless when threatened. A second dorsal fin enables them to swim. It is interesting to watch them glide by.

There is a wide variety of marine life here for both diver and snorkeler to observe. Note that the hard and soft corals harbor a host of small invertebrates such as Christmas tree worms, featherdusters, and flamingo tongues. Nudibranchs, arrow crabs, squirrelfish, trunkfish, damsels, anemones, and sponges also make their home here.

Pillar corals extend their tentacles by day at Pillar Coral Point. Photograph by M. Patoka.

Typical Depth Range:	50–130 feet
Typical Current Conditions:	Minimal
Expertise Required:	Intermediate
Access:	Boat

Peter's Place is a relatively deep mini-wall that is noted for the presence of sea turtles and spotted eagle rays. If turtles and rays tickle your fancy, then this is the site to visit. Peter's Place is situated just to the west of the Bear's Den, on the lee side of the island. The site is defined by the typical spur and groove configuration of the Bay Islands, although there are fewer grooves than spurs here. A mooring buoy is present above a 50-foot deep reef surface. The reef crest then drops to the wall, which bottoms out near 130 feet. Diving profiles usually develop in the 80–100-foot depth range. Upon descent from the mooring line one would proceed the short distance to the wall and there swim to the right.

The highlight of the dive is the splendid vision of green and/or logger-head turtles, and rays. Large spotted eagle rays may reach a weight of 400–500 pounds. They are beautiful, with white circles or spots covering dark bodies. They are commonly observed gliding by in effortless flight, and may be found roaming over reef areas or seagrass beds in search of mollusks, their preferred diet.

If that isn't enough to capture your imagination, the reef is alive with other marine animals. A vast number of tube and barrel sponges siphon plank-

Wrasses flit around coral heads with endless jerky movements.

Sponges come in all shapes and sizes. Some are flexible and some are rigid.

ton-laden water into their bodies. Many of the sponges have other lives sheltered in their protection. A diver glancing inside a sponge should not be surprised to find small gobies, arrow crabs, or shrimp. Above and along the reef are schools of creole wrasses and blue chromis. Black durgeons roam the reef, outfitted in elegant black and white attire.

This is a truly spectacular spot to dive and dive again.

A variety of forms and colors greets the diver in Bay Island waters. Photograph by J. Ford.

Typical Depth Range:	15–130 feet
Typical Current Conditions:	Minimal
Expertise Required:	Novice
Access:	Boat

The Bear's Den is a delightful cave hidden away inside a fabulous mini-wall. A site for everyone, it is east of Half Moon Bay on the north side of the island. Shallow diving and snorkeling, volcanic tunnels, coralline walls and a majestic pinnacle are offered in addition to the Den.

A mooring buoy is present. The top of the reef is 35 feet below the water's surface. Descending the mooring line to the reef crest, a diver will immediately notice a 150-foot-long tunnel. Following the tunnel, the diver will reach the wall, where the depth is about 60 feet. Turn right and swim until the pinnacle is sighted. Upon approach to the pinnacle, the diver should turn right again, ascend to the top of the coral ridge at 15 feet, and then follow the curving ridge to the cave entrance. The cave has a maximum depth of approximately 30 feet. It is a large circular room filled with copper sweepers, crabs, and lobster. A dive light, though not essential, is useful to inspect any nooks and crannies in the cave. The cave has two small dead-end tunnels that can be interesting to examine.

Brain corals are often decorated with exotic Christmas tree worms.

The Bear's Den is an interesting cavern dive. Photograph by M. Patoka.

Coral growth and marine life are abundant here. A variety of sea feathers, sea whips, gorgonians, and lettuce and boulder corals decorate the scenery. Butterflyfish fin slowly from coral to coral, plucking tiny organisms from minute cracks. Butterflyfish are always a favorite to watch. They usually swim in pairs. Many have bands across their eyes or false eye spots that are used for camouflage. An attacking predator may not be able to discern the head from the tail, thereby allowing the butterflyfish to escape.

Sponges

Sponges are usually thought of in terms of bathing. However, sponges are an integral part of the whole coral reef ecosystem. They are the simplest and most primitive of the many-celled animals. Some, like the loggerhead sponge, may be enormous, while others may be no larger than the size of a pea. The skeleton of this type of animal is a network of protein spongin fibers and/or spicules. They are named under the phylum Porifera for the many pores that perforate the animal's skeleton. Particulate matter too small for other animals to feed upon is their mainstay diet. A host of tiny invertebrates such as anemones, crabs, starfish, and shrimp find the inside of the larger sponges a safe haven in which to reside.

5

Diving in Guanaja

Guanaja is surrounded by a narrow zone of reef ridges. The outer bands lure us to spectacular, abruptly plunging drop-offs, Guanaja's own thousand(s)-foot wall. These open-water cliffs combine a crystalline clear sea with rich, colorful, and exotic reef communities. The drop-offs are covered with numerous gorgonians, sea feathers, sponges, and tropical fish. Closer to shore, on the windward side of the island, and eastward of the line of cays, another band of shallower reefs extends the length of the island. Here, coral gardens and mini-cliff overhangs are interspersed with the sand canyon/spur configuration common in the Caribbean.

Majestic pillar corals tower above Bay Island reefs.

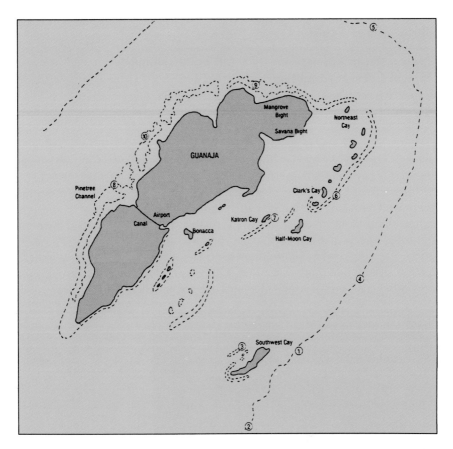

Pillar corals rise majestically from atop the ridges. Landward, individual reef patches infringe on the lagoon system. On the leeward or northern side of the island, a broad band of reef winds its way intermittently down the island's length. This reef is minutes from shore. Caves and tunnels formed by ancient volcanic action twist in intricate patterns. The dive sites outlined capture the essence of diving here: Jim's Silver Lode, Vertigo, Lee's Pleasure, Jado Trader, Caldera del Diablo, Windmill Reef, Katron Cay, Pinnacle, Volcano Caves, and Bayman Bay Drop.

Bay Islands Pillar Coral

Pillar coral (*Dendrogyra cylindrus*) is one of the most statuesque and memorable corals of the Bay Islands. Colonies may form several upright and large cylindrical pillars. Unusual for hard corals, pillar corals extend their long tentacles by day to catch plankton drifting by. If a section of the coral is disturbed, the entire colony contracts its tentacles in a flowing wave.

Jim's Silver Lode

Typical Depth Range:	30 feet to unlimited
Typical Current Conditions:	Minimal
Expertise required:	Intermediate
Access:	Boat

    Jim's Silver Lode is definitely a favorite dive site for divers (and this author). The site is located on the southeast side of Southwest Cay. Dive boats tie up to a permanent buoy to avoid reef damage from anchors.

    Jim's Silver Lode boasts a magnificent wall that drops several thousand feet. Wall crevices are filled with silversides shimmering with sunlight reflected off their hovering forms. To do this site justice, descend from the mooring line to the top of the reef and swim to the wall several yards away. Then descend to approximately 60 feet, follow the wall (on your left) a short distance to a crevice filled with the silversides, glide through the crevice and exit onto a large sandy area at approximately 50 feet. Here you'll

Several crevices interrupt the magnificent wall at Jim's Silverlode.

One of the thrills at Jim's Silver Lode is watching mouth-to-mouth feeding of a barracuda.

be greeted with an array of grouper species, yellowtail snappers, a resident moray eel, and a fat barracuda. This is a feeding station used by local divemasters. You may watch (or help) the divemaster feed the groupers by hand, feed the barracuda mouth to mouth, and hold the moray eel as she feeds on some fishy morsels. Leave the feeding station through a sand canyon and continue your journey down the wall, keeping it to your left until you return to the boat. A variety of outer reef fish are present in quantities to thrill your senses. Queen triggerfish, black durgeons, blackcap basslets, fairy basslets, and butterflyfish are common. Deepwater lace and various sponges extend from the cliff face.

Blackcap basslets belong to the Grammatidae family and are the tiny relatives of groupers and other basses. They are named for the black cap located on their foreheads. A shy, deep-water fish, they are often found in 150-foot depths. This species is one of the distinguishing characteristics of Bay Island diving.

Blackcap basslets hover under ledges. Photograph by M. Patoka.

57

Vertigo

Typical Depth Range:	50 feet to unlimited
Typical Current Conditions:	Variable
Expertise Required:	Intermediate
Access:	Boat

Vertigo lives up to its name! A series of undulating ridges and deep ravines terminate in a several-thousand-foot wall. This site is located on the outer reef band, southwest of Southwest Cay. A mooring buoy is present. The current fluctuates in velocity, therefore, the dive may be planned as either a drift dive or initiated from a stationary point, according to the divemaster's choice. At about 50 feet, you will find yourself on the ridge crests. Beginning the dive from the base of the mooring line, meander up and down the ridges to wind up on the wall, or follow a ridge directly to the wall. If you look closely, you may see five black crinoids majestically waving their arms in the passing current. These sessile members of the starfish family are a rare sight on the reefs, but when observed are usually found attached atop large tub sponges on the ridge crests. Black crinoids have evolved from ancient times. Their bodies are black, but the pinnules (slender arms) are tipped in white. They are exquisitely flowerlike.

Here again, outer reef fish are abundant. Typical inhabitants are black durgeons, orange-spotted filefish, fairy basslets, hogfish, butterflyfish, angelfish, snappers, and jacks. Occasionally, a barracuda may drop in to investigate.

A black crinoid perches regally atop a soft coral at Vertigo.

Lee's Pleasure 3

Typical Depth Range:	5–70 feet
Typical Current Conditions:	Minimal
Expertise Required:	Novice
Access:	Boat

Lee's Pleasure is situated directly behind and north of Southwest Cay, thus sheltered from wind and waves. At this tranquil site there is a mini-wall that begins behind the cay and extends parallel to shore to the island's southwest end. Five feet below the surface the soft corals sway. From there, the wall drops off to a sandy bottom at approximately 70 feet. A mooring buoy is anchored close by the reef. Upon descent from the boat, swim 100 yards to the southwest to encounter the reef, and continue in that direction. To return to the boat, take a reciprocal course.

The shallower depths allow snorkelers and divers to enjoy the array of fish and marine life so plentiful here. Juvenile spotted drums gracefully swim near their hiding spots. A delicately elongated dorsal fin flutters above the drum's body like a ribbon in the wind. Bluebell tunicates are predominant and sought by avid photographers. Interesting coral formations and over-

An orange-spotted filefish prowls the offshore reefs searching for small crustaceans. Photograph by J. Ford.

The mini-wall at Lee's Pleasure is alive with a myriad of fish and invertebrates. Photograph by K. Greenwood.

hangs are found in 30–50-foot depths. Out in the sand, near the mooring buoy is a colony of garden eels. Only their heads and the anterior trunks of their slender bodies poke out from their sandy holes. Garden eels often form permanent colonies. They are territorial and cautious. Here you are also likely to see a spotted eagle ray gliding by, or any of numerous species such as spotted scorpionfish, angelfish, parrotfish, hamlets, Spanish hogfish, damselfish, peacock flounder, seabass, or schools of chromis. Close observation may lead you to spot a strikingly beautiful nudibranch. Sailfin blennies are present, but rarely seen. Look for the blennies in small rocks in the sandy patches. Close by, a beach area is accessible for a picnic and rest between dives.

Arrow crabs are solitary animals that hide in nooks in the coral. Photograph by J. Ford.

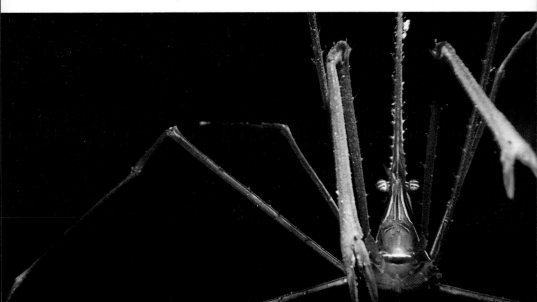

Jado Trader 4

Typical Depth Range:	90–110 feet
Typical Current Conditions:	Variable
Expertise Required:	Advanced
Access:	Boat

Jado Trader is a recently sunk (July 1987) derelict freighter. She lies on her side in 110 feet of water southeast of Southwest Cay and within the outer reef configuration adjacent to a large coral pinnacle. Divers may enjoy both reef and wreck in a single dive. A mooring buoy was established almost directly above the sunken freighter. Initiating the dive from the base of the mooring line, you may swim around and over the wreck, then end the dive ascending the coral pinnacle. The top of the wreck is in 90 feet of water and the head of the pinnacle is 30 feet from the sea's surface.

The Jado Trader *was a derelict freighter that now provides a home for a multitude of grouper species and hogfish.*

The freighter provides the first of artificial substrates in Guanaja, changing an eyesore to new (biologically speaking) marine growth and habitat. Numerous hydroids and algal growth have formed a mat that covers the structure. Doorways and windows give access to a dark, cavernlike shelter for large groupers and hogfish. Near the bow, a black crinoid gathers plankton floating by in the current. A moray eel resides concealed under the safety of the hull.

In addition, a crevice tunnels its way through the adjacent coral pinnacle from a 70-foot depth to the top. At the tip of the pinnacle another black crinoid sits attached to a large sponge. As expected, a variety of marine life harmoniously co-exist here. Besides the large groupers and hogfish are butterflyfish, various seabasses, filefish, surgeonfish, angelfish, wrasses, basslets, arrowcrabs, deepwater lace, and soft corals. One of the seabasses found in the depths is the tobaccofish. This is a small relative of the groupers. Patterned in blotches of brown and orange with a white ventral area, tobaccofish are an interesting species to look for and photograph.

This is an exciting dive for the more experienced diver.

A shy deep-water fish, the tobacco fish cautiously watches divers pass.

Typical Depth Range: 70–140 feet
Typical Current Conditions: Variable
Expertise Required: Advanced
Access: Boat

Breathtaking, heart-stopping, and exciting are words that best describe this site. It is located a fair distance to the north of Northeast Cay on the outer reef band. The surface of the reef starts near a depth of 100 feet and the ravines between spurs bottom out at 140 feet. A mooring buoy is usually present. Rough seas and strong currents are normal. Devil's Cauldron is a rarely visited site because of its distance from Guanaja and its depth, but it is a worthwhile dive nonetheless.

Caldera del Diablo boasts deep offshore pelagic species.

The National Geographic Society recently sponsored research here. Why the interest? During the full moons of January and February, and only during these full moons, thousands upon thousands of fish from the various grouper species leave their usual territories and migrate here. They come to spawn, to propagate a new generation of groupers. Why here, and why only at these times? Researchers are trying to unravel the mystery, but no definitive answers have surfaced.

In addition to the thousands of groupers, sharks cruise slowly and gracefully in the ravines. Hogfish, snappers, large angelfish, and seabasses may also be found. Nearer the surface, schools of horse-eye jacks hover.

Caldera del Diablo is a site that once witnessed can never be forgotten: a superb experience! This reef, however, is not for the novice, and caution is advised even for the experienced.

Spawning season at Caldera del Diablo is an awe inspiring sight when thousands of grouper like this one gather.

Typical Depth Range:	10–70 feet
Typical Current Conditions:	Some surge at reef crest
Expertise Required:	Novice, with divemaster
Access:	Boat

Windmill Reef can be best described as a delightful garden of varying coral formations, sand canyons, and multitudes of fish. The reef is located directly seaward of Clark's Cay. A reef several miles long embraces the chain of cays paralleling Guanaja. Windmill Reef is one of many dive spots within this length of reef. The top of the reef begins in 10 feet of water and dips to 60–70 feet in the sand canyons. A mooring buoy preserves reef structures. Upon descent, the direction to swim is your choice, although a slight current does flow from the northeast in a southwesterly heading.

Lettuce coral form colorful gardens in many areas such as Windmill Reef. Photograph by M. Patoka.

Trumpetfish are usually well camouflaged, often hovering upside down behind soft corals. Photograph by J. Ford.

Fingerlike coral formations reach out to sea. A sand canyon divides each ridge or finger. Here, soft corals sway gently with the currents. Tunicates and sponges ingest plankton-laden water. Numerous fish species dart in and out of holes, observe their surroundings, and feed. Invertebrates patiently wait for prey. A nurse shark sleeps peacefully in one of the sand canyons, hidden under a crevice. Windmill Reef is a photographer's dream. Wrasses, basslets, chromis, damselfish, triggerfish, hamlets, pufferfish, trumpetfish, pillar corals, nudibranchs, arrow crabs, and huge boulder corals are all there for your shutter to catch.

Nudibranchs are without doubt among the most beautiful of all invertebrates inhabiting coral reefs. Coloration is flamboyant and highly decorative. Numerous cerata (ruffled ridges) project from the dorsal area of these elliptically formed animals. Nudibranchs are a shell-less mollusk, usually found (by observant eyes) creeping along the coral on the reef crest. They make wonderful photographic subjects.

Typical Depth Range:	15–70 feet
Typical Current Conditions:	Minimal
Expertise Required:	Novice
Access:	Boat

Katron Cay is a lovely spot of reef located directly seaward from Katron Cay. The reef extends from the eastern to the western ends of the Cay. Situated between the outermost cays and the island of Guanaja, this site provides a diversity of offshore and inshore marine life for your pleasure. It is a popular place for both day and night diving. A mooring buoy is positioned over the wall at the eastern reef edge. The reef crest begins at approximately 15 feet, then descends gradually to 70 feet. Upon entry, a diver ordinarily will drop to the wall and veer right, keeping the wall on the right. Returning to the boat, try swimming near the intersection of the reef the crest and forereef for a different visual perspective. Snorkelers will find this site an enjoyable free-diving thrill.

Glorious overhangs shelter numerous snappers, grunts, and fairy basslets. Impressive coral formations and gardens abound in beauty and color. Small sand canyons interrupt the solidity of coralline walls. Soft corals compete with the brain and boulder corals. With careful observation one can usually find at least one, occasionally a pair, of the elegant juvenile spotted drums.

Overhangs at Katron Cay shelter an array of fish, including the tiny fairy basslets.

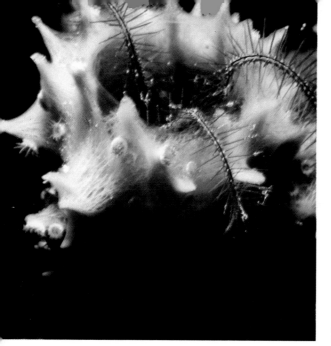

A starfish finds refuge in a sponge. Photograph by J. Ford.

find at least one, occasionally a pair, of the elegant juvenile spotted drums. This is a fascinating, shy member of the drum family. A black smudge is present on the snout. The body is black-and-white barred. In addition, angelfish, sea basses, chromis, parrotfish, filefish, frogfish, and porgies are plentiful. Frogfish can be described as ugly, grotesque, and funny-looking. The first dorsal fin has been modified to look like a fishing lure, which is then used to attract and trap unsuspecting small fish. They are well camouflaged bottom-dwelling fish and prefer shallow water.

This site is a relaxing and rewarding dive for all.

Groupers

Groupers belong to the Serranidae family. Their fusiform shape has been developed for swiftness. Most are bottom or cave dwellers, waiting in lairs for prey to come within range. Many groupers are hermaphroditic, meaning that they begin life being female, produce eggs, then change to male gender at a certain age. Groupers are currently plentiful in the Bay Islands, unlike many other areas where overfishing may have occurred. There is no wealth of data on the reproductive activities of groupers. It is known, however, that during the full moons of January and February, entire populations migrate to spawn at specific locations in the Caribbean. Two known sites in the Bay Islands are offshore Guanaja and Barbareta.

Pinnacle 8

Typical Depth Range:	15–130 feet
Typical Current Conditions:	Minimal
Expertise Required:	Intermediate
Access:	Boat

    This spot is aptly named, for it is indeed a pinnacle of coral that rises several feet away from the main reef structure. Pinnacle is on the lee side of Guanaja, situated near the mouth of Pine Tree Channel, across from Soldado Beach. It is near the mini-wall, which stretches the length of the island's lee side. The tip of the pinnacle starts in 52 feet of water and plunges to a sandy bottom at 130 feet. A mooring buoy is present on the main reef structure. You descend 15 feet down the mooring line to the reef crest, then out to the wall, turning left, and then swim a short distance to sight the Pinnacle ahead. Roaming around the Pinnacle, you will encounter a small crevice that

Grouper are still plentiful in the Bay Islands. This one eyes the diver curiously.

Excellent water clarity heightens the diving experience. Photograph by J. Ford.

bisects the Pinnacle at 80 feet. Entering the crevice on a sunny day is similar to entering a snowflake-encrusted forest. Contained within is a fairy-tale land of black coral that is transformed by the sunlight above into shimmering white lace!

Groupers collect here and wait patiently for dive guides to feed them. A large, green moray eel resides king-of-the-mountain style at the top of the Pinnacle and curiously watches divers glide by. For fish enthusiasts, fairy and blackcap basslets hover under ledges. Sharpnose pufferfish, angelfish, snappers, and butterflyfish are also seen. Vase sponges reach out from their perches.

On the neighboring reef, scores of fish species feed, reproduce, and defend their territories. Occasionally, a yellow-phase coney can be spotted. Soft corals abound. Pillar corals pop up everywhere in impressive array. Don't miss this dive!

Black Rocks (Volcano Caves) 9

Typical Depth Range:	6–60 feet
Typical Current Conditions:	Minimal
Expertise Required:	Novice, with divemaster
Access:	Boat

   The Black Rocks are located on the lee side of Guanaja, northeast from the village of Mangrove Bight. Volcanic in origin, this intricate maze of cliffs, caverns, and tunnels is like none other found in Guanaja. The caves are one of the most popular dive sites and often requested by visiting divers. Black Rocks is a 1½-mile-long wall with cave after cave penetrating its exterior.
   No mooring buoy is present, so anchors are dropped in a sandy patch adjacent to the caves. The top of the reef begins less than 10 feet from the surface and drops to 60 feet at the base. You should descend down the anchor line to the sandy area below to begin the dive there. It is strongly recommended that you follow a divemaster or knowledgeable guide through the caves' intricate maze.

A rich growth of soft coral populates the reefs, giving each its own character.

A diver can spend hours meandering leisurely through the complex maze of tunnels at Black Rocks.

Due to the geologic structure of the caves that prohibits extensive coral growth, fish life is not as abundant as elsewhere. You will find this a trivial irritation, however, in comparison to the splendor of the cave structures. Marine life to be found includes soft and hard corals, damselfish, butterflyfish, masked gobies, squirrelfish, an occasional nurse shark, and copper sweepers. Copper sweepers are a deep-bodied, compressed fish. Hues of silver and copper cover their bodies, hence their name (they are also known as glassy sweepers). Copper sweepers prefer the darkness of caves, and appear to be nocturnal in nature.

Typical Depth Range: 10–100 feet
Typical Current Conditions: Minimal
Expertise Required: Novice
Access: Boat

Bayman Bay Drop is located just beyond the continuous reef structure on the leeward side of Guanaja. Looking down from the reef crest/forereef interphase, you can see straight into a plunging drop-off of inverted coralline overhangs. Numerous tunnels and caverns have been carved by timeless water action throughout the site. It is a fabulous dive for anyone, novice to advanced. Snorkelers will enjoy the marine life inhabiting the reef crest and upper forereef.

Butterflyfish are marked with extra "eyes," bands, or spots to confuse predators. They often swim in pairs, and they mate for life. Photograph by J. Ford.

Glorious inverted coralline overhangs and tunnels characterize Bayman Bay Drop.

A mooring buoy sits over the reef crest. It is a short swim to the wall from the buoy. At the wall, head to the right. Only fin kicks away is a crevice covered with coralline growth, which is worth peeking into. The top of the reef is just a few feet below the surface, and the wall drops sharply to approximately 100 feet. Towering islands of corals narrowly separated from the wall form enticing tunnels. Boulder coral shaped like shingles predominates here. Huge barrel sponges and azure vase sponges dot the scenery. An array of fish dart and hide among these impressive configurations. Schools of creole wrasses may surround a diver, as blue runner jacks race by. Indigo hamlets, parrotfish, butterflyfish, masked gobies, fairy basslets, sharpnose pufferfish, and angelfish abound. Tunicates cling to the corals, ingesting plankton-rich water.

Tunicates

Tunicates are probably among the least-mentioned and least-noticed animals on the reefs. Belonging to the lower vertebrates, they possess a primitive rodlike backbone in infancy, which evolves into a cellulose external covering called a "tunic." Their bodies usually appear in the form of a bunch of grapes. Although some are drab, most exhibit a dazzling array of colors. Look for them in the shallower waters.

The tunicate can be a superb photographic subject.

6

Diving in Barbareta

Barbareta is a mountainous, wildly beautiful, and privately owned island. Few people live on Barbareta and few buildings spoil the natural wooded landscape. One has the feeling that there are parts of the island that have never been visited by man.

In past years, there was a resort on the island, but it has been closed for some time, and no information about staying there is available at the time of this publication.

The island's allure for divers is the spectacular Morat Wall, which is described in detail for the benefit of advanced divers who are looking for something really special. Fortunately, even though the resort is closed, charter trips to the wall from Roatan and Guanaja can be arranged. Even for the nondiver, the boat ride out to Barbareta as a passenger on a chartered dive boat would be worthwhile just for the scenery. You can also snorkel and picnic around the nearby Pigeon Cays.

Black coral line the walls at Barbareta in profusion; harvesting it is illegal by Honduran law.

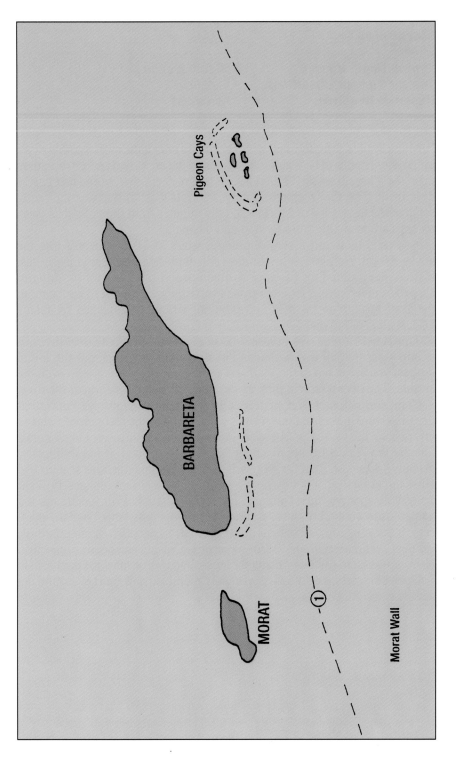

MORAT

BARBARETA

Pigeon Cays

Morat Wall

①

Morat Wall

Typical Depth Range:	50 feet to unlimited
Typical Current Conditions:	Variable
Expertise Required:	Advanced
Access:	Boat

Morat Wall is definitely and without a doubt one of the most exciting dives in the Bay Islands. The water is so blue and the coral reefs so pristine they take one's breath away. The reef is so magnificent that words can barely describe it. The site is approximately one mile west of Barbareta, directly south of the tiny island of Morat, and only minutes from shore. Special charter trips are available from Roatan and Guanaja.

A several-thousand-foot wall plunges from 50–70-foot depths into the abyss. Morat Wall boasts a fabulous cliff with few sand canyons. It has, instead, foot after foot of coral overhangs and a solid wall of shingle-shaped boulder corals. Isolated from overfishing abuse due to its location, the Wall appears to be wild and pristine, virtually untouched by man's nets, spears, or knives.

This is a drift dive. No mooring buoy is present. As in all drift dives, it is important that all divers descend and ascend together. From the initial descent you swim out to the Wall and simply and effortlessly drift with the current. The dive boat will pick up everyone at the completion of the dive.

Coral formations tower majestically and sand canyon/spur configurations interrupt the continuous wall of coral. Most of the recognized fish and invertebrate life of the Caribbean are present here. A profusion of black corals line the Wall at depths approaching 90 feet and beyond. Hawksbill turtles placidly swim past. En route, you will be greeted with numerous seafans and other soft corals, pillar corals, deepwater lace, huge basket sponges, brilliant azure vase sponges, tube sponges, and basket starfish. Fish species are too numerous to count, but those commonly seen include large hogfish, snappers, black durgeons, Groupers of all species, tobaccofish, harlequin bass, hamlets, reef butterflyfish (a rarity), parrotfish, queen and ocean triggerfish, blackcap basslets, rainbow runners, filefish, and even a sunshine damselfish.

Upon completion of the dive, you may picnic on and snorkel around the nearby small Pigeon Cays.

Morat Wall plunges abruptly into the abyss. ▶

7

Diving in Cayos Cochinos (Hog Islands)

The Cayos Cochinos are a group of eleven small cays, with Cochinos Grande being the largest. Cochinos Grande and the other cays are encircled by well-developed narrow bands of fringing reefs. There are several deeper reef structures to the north of the islands. All are covered with soft corals, lobster, various hard corals, sponges, groupers, turtles, and tunicates. The area is rarely visited by nonnatives, leaving the reefs virtually pristine. You will find wonderful diving anywhere along these reefs in both shallow

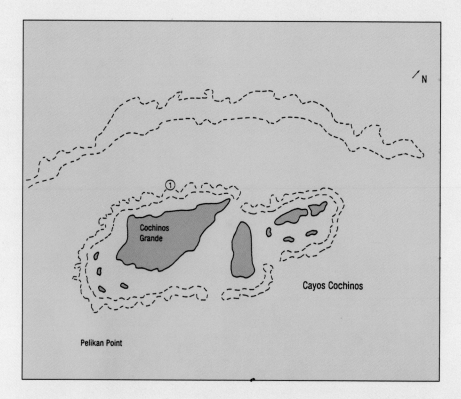

A rainbow of color awaits an adventurous diver at the Cayos Cochinos. Photograph by M. Patoka.

and deep water. The typical sand/ridge configurations are constructed in the reef face. Pinnacles, overhangs, and ledges dot the reef landscape. The sites are almost unexplored; one might even name a site. Only one site will be described and depicted in this book. A visit to the Cayos Cochinos enables the adventurous diver to experience reefs hardly touched by man and to have the pleasure of diving a pristine area in solitude. Tunicates are prolific and await the photographer's shutter.

Pelikan Point Wall

Typical Depth Range:	5–110 feet
Typical Current Conditions:	Minimal
Expertise Required:	Novice
Access:	Boat

Pelikan Point Wall is a superb, sheer cliff of coral, sand canyons, enormous overhangs of dripping corals, and small caverns. The site, on a wall running in a westerly-northwesterly direction, is located only minutes from shore off Cochinos Grande.

You descend from the boat down to the reef crest less than 10 feet from the surface. A short swim to the Wall brings you face to face with a sheer drop-off. The Wall drops almost vertically 100 feet. Angling to the right against the current you may then proceed at a pace of your choosing; of course, the slower you proceed, the more there is to see, and there are overhangs to swim under and caverns to investigate.

Enormous mounds of boulder coral form the backbone of many reefs.

Only in maturity do the blue tangs become blue. When young, they are a brilliant yellow.

Marine life is diverse and abundant. It might be possible to see a seahorse or two in quiet, calm spots on the reef crest. Tunicates are clustered everywhere. Boulder corals change shape from rounded spires to the deeper water formation of shingled plates. Juvenile spotted drums shelter under ledges. Arrow crabs and anemones find refuge under rocks and in cracks. Groupers quietly await prey close to the caves and overhangs. Trunkfish, doctorfish, grunts, and possibly a scorpionfish or two co-exist in harmony. Trunkfish and cowfish belong to the Ostraciidae family. Their bodies are more or less triangular in shape and are armored with bony plates. Cowfish receive their name from the spine that projects from each eye. They are generally found in shallow waters over reefs or seagrass beds.

8

Diving in Utila

Utila's reefs are for the most part unexplored by visitors. Locals from the mainland of Honduras and commercial lobster divers frequent the reefs here. The reefs are both inshore and offshore from the island, and are situated primarily to the west and southwest. Diving from shore is possible. The offshore reefs produce an abundance of aquatic life that has been rather left alone by man. Black and elkhorn coral forests are magnificent. Coral formations tower over sandy bottoms. Coral gardens show off their colors. Reefs beginning at a depth of 5 feet may drop sharply to 200 feet. For the diver

Snappers and porkfish are a common sight near tunnels and caves. Photograph by J. Ford.

who wants a true adventure and doesn't need fancy boats and accommodations or mapped dive sites, this is the place to visit. No individually named sites are presented here, but that does not indicate a lack of exotic and delightful dive opportunities. It does indicate that a visitor to Utila becomes an explorer, discovering sites for him- or herself.

Sea Turtles

Potentially a vanishing breed of marine life in the Bay Islands, sea turtles historically have been hunted for meat, and for the carapace, which is used to make jewelry. Presently, turtles are protected throughout much of the world and in the Bay Islands. It is illegal to capture any one of the species for commercial use. There are three commonly observed sea turtles in the Bay Islands, the green, hawksbill, and loggerhead. Each is characterized by a large oval-shaped carapace and paddlelike limbs. They mate in shallow water close to a beach, where the females then migrate to lay hundreds of eggs in the sand. Turtles are a highlight of any dive. However, you should use caution when approaching a turtle because turtles do bite. Also, if you try to hold onto one, you may find yourself being dragged rapidly downward, resulting in injury to yourself or the turtle.

Sea turtles are protected throughout the Bay Islands. Photograph by J. Ford.

9

Smart, Safe Diving

Each dive can be a safe and enjoyable experience. It is entirely up to you to make your dives a lasting, pleasurable memory.

The following is a helpful list of safe diving practices.

Never Dive Alone. Always dive with a buddy, preferably someone knowledgeable of the selected dive spot and diving practices. Try not to dive with someone unknown.

Breathe Properly. Never hold your breath while diving. Always breathe. Breathing should be slightly deeper and slower than normal.

Know Your Limitations. Know what your limitations are, and don't force yourself beyond what you can comfortably perform.

Maintain Good Mental and Physical Condition. Don't dive if tired or feeling ill.

Be Well Trained. Don't dive unless certified by a licensed dive instructor.

Know Decompression Tables. Know how to read the tables, plan the dives accordingly, and understand emergency methods.

Use Correct, Proper, Functioning Dive Gear. Always check all gear prior to leaving on a trip and prior to a dive.

Ascend Correctly. Look up while ascending, breathe regularly, and do not ascend faster than 60 feet per minute.

Have a Safety Stop. Stop at 15 feet for 2 or 3 minutes prior to exiting the water.

Reef Etiquette and Buoyancy Control

While moorings may go a long way toward reducing anchor damage to our reefs, so far there is nothing to protect reefs from damage by divers . . . except divers. Dive sites tend to be located where the reefs and walls display the most beautiful corals and sponges. And it only takes a moment—an inadvertently placed hand or knee on the coral or an unaware brush or kick with a fin—to destroy this fragile living part of our delicate ecosystem. Luckily, it only takes a little extra preparation and consideration to preserve it for generations of divers to come.

So if you're a new diver, a little rusty after a long hiatus on dry land, diving with new equipment . . . or if you just haven't paid much attention to your reef etiquette and buoyancy control in the past, here are a few helpful tips how you can personally help preserve our underwater environment:

Weight Yourself Properly. Never dive with too much weight. (Northern divers—this means you! When you put on a lighter wetsuit or dive skin, shed some of those lead pounds, too!) Weight yourself so that you *float at eye level* on the surface with your lungs full of air and none in your BCD. Exhale fully and you should begin to sink. As your week of diving goes by and you relax underwater, drop some more weight. Ask your divemaster what kind of tank you're using. Tanks vary in their buoyancy when they are empty. You want to be able to hover comfortably at 15 feet to make your safety stop when your tank is low at the end of your dive.

Control Your Buoyancy with Your Breathing. If you are properly weighted and have successfully attained neutral buoyancy with your BCD at depth, you should be able to fine-tune your hovering capacity by inhaling and exhaling. Being able to rise and sink at will is the real trick to being able to hover, float, and glide over and around the reef formations with grace and skill.

Avoid Fin Damage to Coral. Never stand (or kneel) on the corals. If you're hovering above the reef, keep your fins up off the reef. If you're swimming, do so in a horizontal position looking down so you're not flutter-kicking the reef. When you're cruising through a narrow space such as a tunnel or gully between coral heads, keep an eye on where your feet are and, if necessary, make your kicks small and efficient to move through the compact area. Reef etiquette also demands that if you are swimming near a sandy bottom, stay several feet above the sand so you don't kick up any silt and ruin the dive for other divers.

Don't Touch the Reef. No matter how pretty and tempting the coral and sponges are, look but don't touch. And never, never grab onto the reef to steady yourself. If you need to stabilize yourself or keep from bumping into things or other divers, try using one or two fingers instead of your entire hand. And look for dead spots, areas between the corals or even the underside of a coral cranny where there is generally less growth.

Watch Where You Land. If you need to touch down or kneel on solid ground, look for a sandy area in between the coral heads. If you need to take a photo, float or glide over your subject or steady yourself with a finger, but keep the rest of your body away from the reef. If you can't get the picture or see your subject without lying on the coral . . . don't take the picture!

Don't Drag Loose Gauges or Octopus Across the Reef. Hanging consoles, goody bags, tools, and other unsecured equipment can do as much damage to the corals as your hands and feet. Keep your equipment close to your body by tucking them into your BC pockets or using retainer clips. You can even put your console between your tank and your back.

Don't Grab the Marine Creatures. Don't ride the turtle, grab the lobsters, chase the stingrays, or harass the eels. They are curious by nature and will gradually move toward you if you leave them alone. If you grab them, they'll disappear faster than you can clear your mask . . . and no one else will have the chance to see them either.

Be considerate. Leave the reef in the same condition in which you found it. In this way it will remain healthy and thriving for future divers to enjoy.

The Ocean Charter*

The oceans belong to no one, they belong to all of us, so they belong to me. It is my ocean, my sea, my water. I am a warden of this wilderness. All the creatures that dwell there are part of my responsibility, everyone's responsibility.

We who live on land have everything to do with the sea even if we have nothing to do with it directly. By being responsible for the oceans we are responsible for the quality of our lives and quality of life of other living things for now and in the future.

The ocean is important to all of us. We must treat the ocean as something precious that belongs to us. Though we cannot own it nor possess it, it is ours to protect and preserve, to use wisely and with care, to enjoy and explore. We must claim the ocean for the good of all living creatures.

I proclaim, as each of us must proclaim: These are my waters. I pledge myself as a warden of the wilderness, a guardian of nature, vanguard of the ocean realm, and sentinel of the seas.

It is my ocean.

* From "Oceans in Peril," by John Christopher Fine. Used with permission.

Appendix: Diving and Snorkeling Operations

The resorts and dive boats cited here are included as an aid to the reader. The author has made an effort to include all known operations at the time of publication. This presentation does not favor any operation nor does it constitute an endorsement of these resorts. If operators/owners wish to be included in future reprints/editions, please contact Pisces Books, P.O. Box 2608, Houston, Texas, 77252-2608.

Roatan

Anthony's Key Resort
1385 Coral Way
Suite 401
Miami, FL 33145
305-858-3483
800-227-3483

Casas de la Playa Roatan
c/o Tino Monterosso
414-582-4806

Cay View Resort
800-354-3483
713-558-2596

CocoView Resort
P.O. Box 877
San Antonio, FL 33576-0877
800-282-8932

Fantasy Island Beach Resort
304 Plant Avenue
Tampa, FL 33606
800-6-ROATAN
813-251-5771
FAX 011-504-45-1222

Reed's Beach House
6591 Lasley Shore Dr.
Winneconne, WI 54986
414-582-4155

Reef House Resort
P.O. Box 40331
San Antonio, TX 78229
800-328-8897
512-681-2888

Romeo's Resort
2901 N.E. 23rd Court
Pompano Beach, FL 33062
800-535-3483
305-942-6073

Sunrise Hotel
800-328-5285

Cayos Cochinos

Plantation Beach Resort
515 S.W. 1st Avenue
Ft. Lauderdale, FL 33301
800-628-3723

Live Aboards

Bay Islands Aggressor
P.O. Drawer K
Morgan City, LA 70381
504-385-2416

Isla Mia
800-874-7636
FAX 011-504-45-1478

Roatan Charter, Inc.
P.O. Box 877
San Antonio, FL 33576
800-282-8932

Guanaja

Bayman Bay Club
11750 N.W. 19th St.
Plantation, FL 33323
305-370-2120
1-800-524-1823

Casa Sobre el Mar
1-800-869-7295

Club Guanaja Este
P.O. Box 40541
Cincinnati, OH 45240
513-825-3845
FAX 011-504-45-4145

Diving Place "Above and Below"
c/o Hans Weller
Fruit Harbor Bight
Guanaja, Bay Islands
Honduras CA

Nautilus Dive Resort
Sandy Bay, Guanaja, Bay Islands,
Honduras CA
512-863-9079
800-535-7063
FAX 011-504-45-4135

Posada del Sol
1201 U.S. Highway #1
Suite 220
North Palm Beach, FL 33408
800-642-DIVE
407-624-3483